MOMENTS OF GRACE

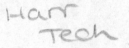

ELIZABETH JENNINGS

Moments of Grace

Carcanet·Manchester

For Richard Pasco
and Barbara Leigh Hunt

SBN 85635 281 0

First published in 1979 by
Carcanet New Press Limited
330 Corn Exchange Buildings
Manchester M4 3BG

The publisher acknowledges the financial assistance of
the Arts Council of Great Britain.

Printed in Great Britain by Billings, Guildford

CONTENTS

7   Into the Hour
8   An Answer to Odd Advice
9   A Meditation in March 1979
10 The Sermon of Appearances
11 Among Farm Workers
12 To be a Sunflower
13 Cypresses
14 Outside Greece
15 The Whole Bestiary
16 Flies
17 Goldfinch
18 Friesian Cows
19 Rook
20 Cat in Winter
21 The Shoot
22 A Beseeching
23 Watcher
24 A Christmas Carol for 1978
25 Forgiveness
26 Never Such Peace
27 The Way of it
28 Channel Port Night
29 A Weather Spell
30 Thought and Feeling
31 I Count the Moments
32 Love Needs an Elegy
33 On its Own
34 Death
35 An Elusive One
36 Haunted House
37 Spirits
38 The Dangerous Ones
39 Spell of the Elements
40 A Chorus of Creation

6]

41   A Chorus
42   An Education
43   A New Patience
44   Euthenasia
45   The Wrong Subject
46   Some Never Forgotten Words of my Mother's
47   The Gardens Stretch
48   Summer Scene
49   Sea Song
50   Sea-Drunk
51   Spring Twilight
52   Night Moment
53   Night Power
54   The Apt Phrase
55   A Proustian Moment
56   A Chinese Poem
57   Braque's Dream
58   Christmas Suite in Five Movements
     1. The Fear
     2. The Child
     3. A Litany
     4. The Despair
     5. The Victory

INTO THE HOUR

I have come into the hour of a white healing.
Grief's surgery is over and I wear
The scar of my remorse and of my feeling.

I have come into a sudden sunlit hour
When ghosts are scared to corners. I have come
Into the time when grief begins to flower

Into a new love. It had filled my room
Long before I recognized it. Now
I speak its name. Grief finds its good way home.

The apple-blossom's handsome on the bough
And Paradise spreads round. I touch its grass.
I want to celebrate but don't know how.

I need not speak though everyone I pass
Stares at me kindly. I would put my hand
Into their hands. Now I have lost my loss

In some way I may later understand.
I hear the singing of the summer grass.
And love, I find, has no considered end,

Nor is it subject to the wilderness
Which follows death. I am not traitor to
A person or a memory. I trace

Behind that love another which is running
Around, ahead. I need not ask its meaning.

AN ANSWER TO ODD ADVICE

You who would have me often cynical
And even bitter, have you never thought
I have my moments of pure anger bought
Always highly? In my lyrical
Verse you doubtless find what you have sought,

A childishness. You should know it is hard
To keep the clear eye and the trust in men.
I have met cruelty but then, again,
I've found the good more often. I am scarred,
Like others, after unjust charges. When

You tell me to be disillusioned, I
Answer, 'I've tried and never yet succeeded
And I am glad I have not.' Hope is needed
If in a dark world some, like me, will try
To last through mankind's new Gethsemane

And be near any Christ again who's pleaded
For friends, for comfort, and not yet to die.

A MEDITATION IN MARCH 1979

No bravery, no trumpets' festival,
Death is a little circumstance. Our wars
Are scattered, cold, a shadow of us all
And of our lack of awe and tact. We go
Under the neon-lights, under the show
Of signals, barricades, Iron Curtains too.
And we diminish what we mean and are
And crave a comfort out of fashion now.
We eye the spaces which once lit a star
To light the world. Children run wild and how
Are we to tame them who have built Misrule?
Love was a master, now it is a fool.

And grace is caught in seconds unexpected—
Beads of light hung on a chain of stars,
The child's goodnight look. All the recollected
Dead who fill our shelves. They wrote their lives.
They lived by law, but we are otherwise.
Rhodesia, China, Persia are at odds
And so are we. What is important is
That, lacking faith, we do not place false gods
Upon our shaky thrones. Believers claim
They know a God and dare to speak his name.
We need belief and so we put it in
Our children. We invest too much in them.
They turn with scornful eyes and they are right.
The stars hang in old patterns, death so near
Seems just accomplished on the edge of night.
We can reach out and almost touch its hem.
And what is happening in Jerusalem?

THE SERMON OF APPEARANCES

We are motes dancing,
We are flecks of the rainbow settling down
For a definite twelve hours.
We are appearances,
We are decorators.
We take the elements for frivolous reasons.
We are the bonus seasons.

Chips from a huge bonfire, we are. We are
Today what stars are to the night but better,
Believe that. It is true.
We are the tan on you
And the healthy feel caught in a summer sea
Or under southern tree after tree.

Glittering on a coming tide, we run
According to our own
Rules. We have them.
What is it we teach?
The value of appearances, the prize
Of a moment. We can give you Midas hands
But remember, always, the price.
We give you different eyes
And remorseless beginnings and ends.

AMONG FARM WORKERS

My hands hang loose like gloves a child has.
They're tied through sleeves and won't be lost. Mine are.
I would have work to roughen them, would press
On spade or hoe. Instead, these hands hang here

As I stroll through the country of a season
Not spring, not winter. Yet what work I pass—
Digging that ditch, for instance, felling trees.
Instead my hands are hand-cuffs in a prison,

The prison being me. I smell, I taste
The curdling country air but there is no
Work for me. I can't join with the rest

Who smell of labour. Envious, I watch grow
Catkins hanging in the wind. What waste
Walks with me. Yet I reap who never sow.

TO BE A SUNFLOWER

    To be a sunflower, to
Smile on the sad gardeners, to be
    Admired and grow
As cipher of that face which finally
      Will be the death of me.

    To look up aslant
At the feasting sun, sun worn as a dress
    By me. I can't, no, can't
Believe my skin will shrivel, that winds will toss
      Even the tallest of us.

    I exercise my flesh-
Bound spirit with this freedom of a flower
    Large but never lush.
It bends with dignity, will never cower
      But quietly heel over.

CYPRESSES

Those definite proportions, those strong shapes,
Are yet among the randomness of things.
The oxen plough on as the tourist sleeps
And in that sleep dreams the cypress is
A shadow-thrower, and the dark it keeps
Is the pure essence of all cypresses.

So in that stalwart upward-turning tree,
That looking-cool black candle with no flame,
We can behold the whole of Tuscany.
Turn to your window as the small hours sound
A spell of time, and under pale stars claim
A score of cypresses shading the ground.

Cyphers of a language we don't need
To learn. It is no lost Etruscan now
Decoded. It's by signs that these trees plead.
They are steadfast, true until you stare.
Then many shadows throng and form and bow
In cypress-surfeited and Tuscan air.

In Renaissance paintings only these
Cypresses stay stark, definite and climb
One by one, a company of trees
Giving bonus landscapes whose fore-view
Is the attraction. In and out of time
Cypress and shadow step away from you.

OUTSIDE GREECE

    Out of the city quickly. There it is—
Pastoral Greece a thousand years ago.
    The air is clear, the sea keeps changing, changing,
Spendthrift alteration of all blues.
    And greens also. Be still and listen here.

    The light embraces you and there are voices
Far away at first and then all round
    Like an invisible pantheon, all gods
Subdued a little. Dryads might walk out
    Of pines surrounding Epidaurus. What

    Do clockless voices say that bears upon
Our world? They speak of death and love and fate.
    How bleak that wisdom was in this warm air,
Or did the Greeks turn Puritan among
    Such natural riches? It could be, it could.

    Poor land for farmers. Every tithe of land
Is planted. See, a goat herd blocks the way.
    The sun puts out its arms and presses us
To odd conclusions. Air seems much like earth.
    Greece mixes up the elements and we
Know ancient people back to our own birth.

THE WHOLE BESTIARY

Here they come, wandering, slipping, striding, looming,
The whole *Bestiary* into a world beginning,
    A life to jaunt about on this one globe
Known to be peopled among the galaxies, nebulae,
    Southern Cross, all the wide lap of space.

And the beasts are waiting for us, a whole rôle,
Parrot gossips, birds try maiden wings,
    All separate, each is another world,
A pulse of life, the one gift shared in common—
    Determination to last. Here we breathed in life,

And breathed on life and approved
The animals, birds, contained in their own substance,
    Gripped by their own element,
These are savage for life, while we examine
    The look and feel of a world of a thousand textures,
Of seething appeals to the five expert senses.

Here we are, and we are on the threshold
Of the reason why life needs death, of the reason why love
    Needs suffering over and over.
The world is maimed and the *Bestiary* is shadowed
    But it is, some believe, the shadow of a Creator
Brooding over his business with us, attentive
    To the first choice we make.

FLIES

All through the winter these tunnel
Torpid air, desert of central heating,
Doubling men's thirst. These live God
Knows where, and they are his creatures.
Buzz, buzz, they insist,
Flies fallen from summer,
Jig-zagging from cupboards, appearing
At the first left toffee,
And the smoking Christmas cake.

They carry dirt, we know,
They are ugly. They cannot help it.
Aesop would have a message. Creatures are good
For our metaphorical questions
And our necessary teaching.
I will try to admire this toss of a cigarette burning,
Bringing destruction and pain
But being so dogged with it.
'Let the flies come still,' I say
And let no one else complain.

GOLDFINCH

These claws too contain
A bad crop. The goldfinch preys on the blossom
Of apple, that froth and tide of a white
Spring wedding. The neatness, the tailor-made
Touch of his suit bespeaks a harmlessness,
A wish to please that he is stranger to.

Why must we pet the world's destroyers?
I am not speaking of the soft-handed cream-buyers
Or the vendors of fresh liver
To fill the guts of a cat, no, I speak
A contradiction. I praise the pluck of the goldfinch
But I abhor this lamentable *gourmet*
Who plucks from the Eden branch the Eden flower,
Such a bright appearance, such a dandy to the inch.

FRIESIAN COWS

Muddy-booted and with an acrobatic way
With churns and electric milker,
He calls the litany of these docile Friesians
Who wait with a world's patience to have their milk
Sucked from their bloated udders.

I can, at this distance,
With the memory of the cowman's 'Honey, Snowdrop',
Understand entirely the vegetarian.
More, I can see the point
Of the 'Protection of Animals' people,

'But let them be milked,' I say, 'But not misused,
Let the cow keep her calf for longer than
A day . . .' You interrupt and you are right.
'My child needs that milk.' I stammer
'I'm sorry,' and go away with a dream of milkers
Grazing in Paradise. I have shut the gate.

ROOK

Lover of natural sky-scrapers, builder in
Face of East winds, and any winds indeed,
Acrobat whose tight-rope is a branch,
And a thin one at that, you survey
The stripes of fields, clutch of cottages here,
And there the factories with their blinds and humming,
There, a motor-way.

No one has called you king of anything,
You rook, you wary traveller, you who don't
Know what vertigo is. Why haven't we admired you
Before? Being a rook is a daring thing
But height and distance are your media,
You evening-dressed, almost haphazard bird.
A little nearer to the sun you are
Than us. You could be photographed by a star.

CAT IN WINTER

Evader mostly, a glancing cold, a watcher
Of snow from a warm distance, a clever seeker
Of the heated corner, the generous lap, the fingers
Handing tit-bits or filling a shallow saucer—

So the cat in winter and his movements.
He slinks into hiding places like a dandy
Recovering from a party or preparing
For another appearance in the evening. This one,
Striped, ginger and handsome,

Is a teller of weather, has a machine in his head
Which is a barometer to him. He is inventive,
Enterprising always, always lucky.
We sink into February and its inertia.
The cat's ears are cocked for a spring of happy hunting.

THE SHOOT

They are bringing the bright birds down.
The winter trees are shaken, the sky looks on
    And, far away, a town
Writes its houses on a sky with no sun.
    They are bringing the bright birds down.

    And from my room I can see
Patches of snow which the thaw hasn't reached yet,
    And now I seem to be
Alone. The wind goes off. What birds wait,
    Birds I cannot see?

    And then anger comes on fast.
I storm inwardly at these cold men
    Who will be glad to have passed
An afternoon giving the bright birds pain
    And a violent death at last.

    They are bringing the bright birds down.
Yesterday's pheasant will plummet through the air.
    And I am not guiltless, I own,
For I have eaten pheasants who shelter here.
    I too have brought them down.

A BESEECHING

    Lord, they suffer, still they suffer,
Lord of the long hills and low fields and the flat
Meadows, Lord of little places, weather
Seldom extreme. Lord, Christ, your heart
Beats in this country. You have gathered together
    Us and what we would offer.

    Lord, we are bold in sin,
Rich in hoardings, fencing your Presence out.
Move in our hearts, we can be kindly, be
The moon to our tide of passion, take our doubt
Down to the rock and the everlasting sea
    Where another world will begin.

WATCHER

He is the watcher underneath the stars.
He dresses the dome of night with strings of long
   Meditations. He seldom moves. If he does,
It is to become acquainted with nightly creatures
   And now with hibernators who are creeping
Out of their snowy sleep, their habitations
   Which, perilously, just kept them warm enough.
The watcher is handy and burly but even he

Rejoices in his own silence at the change
Apparent everywhere as the glacier winter
   Slides away, as the woken grass speaks
And a chorus of thrushes and blackbirds sings the hours.
   This watcher joins them in his meditations:
But he thinks of a shadow only just beginning
   To creep over grass dressed by the sun.
It is the encroachment of a gallows-tree.
   And the watcher waits for the torment in a garden,
Eden swept out, and a dark figure weeping.

A CHRISTMAS CAROL FOR 1978

Again it comes as if
   It never was before—
This trumpet-sound of life,
   This weakness to adore.

God is not hidden when
   This birth takes place again,
O we are unkind men
   But in this—God-made-Man

Who needs us—we use all
   We still have of our best,
To this child's hungry call
   We offer him our trust.

Holly is bleeding, wise
   Men have started out
Upon their enterprise,
   And we have no more doubt,

For Mary sings again,
   Again to the locked heart,
We open it with pain,
We play our Christmas part.

FORGIVENESS

Anger, pity, always, most, forgive.
It is the word which we surrender by,
It is the language where we have to live,

For all torn tempers, sulks and brawls at last
Lie down in huge relief as if the world
Paused on its axis. Sorrow does sound best

When whispered near a window which can hold
The full moon or its quarter. Love, I say,
In spite of many hours when I was cold

And obdurate I never meant to stay
Like that or, if I meant to, I can't keep
The anger up. Our storms must draw away,

Their durance is not long. Almost asleep,
I listen now to winds' parley with trees
And feel a kind of comforting so deep

I want to share it. This unpaid-for peace
Possesses me. How much I wish to give
Some back to you, but living's made of these

Moments when every anger comes to grief
And we are rich in right apologies.

NEVER SUCH PEACE

Never such peace before, never such rest
As when, a gaze away from summer sky
We watched the bleeding and the burning west.
We did not move, we did not even sigh.
Your hand lay on my breast.

And in that centre, as it were, of calm,
It was as if the acts which we had done
Were flared out in the west. The night was warm
And in this personal peace we saw a sun
That burns but does not harm.

Not what you did or what I said's the drift
Now. I remember silence as the light
Seeped down the sky and you and I were left.
It was not day still and it was not night
When we, though sleep-bereft,

Watched an epic sunset, did not move
But stared out at the final act but one.
The elements were copying our love
And dramatising our small union,
And nobody moved off.

A curtain fell, the night's, so slow to come
We did not notice it until the air,
The outer star-packed air flowed through the room.
And when you pointed at one bigger star
Both of us were dumb.

THE WAY OF IT

When it is over or before it starts,
    We know the strength of love.
It is so cool, this literature of hearts.
It lies in books. Only the pages move.

When blood is beating and the pulse unsteady
    And eyes are gladly blurred,
When nouns we use are quite inept but ready,
We lose the wish for any nerveless word.

And yet, and yet, our whispered passion tells
    Us that we should claim
A speech, a part. But we are somewhere else
And where we are is mapless with no name.

When fire is ashes and the hearth shows no
    Burning we start to tell
Our history but cannot make it glow
Even though what we know we know so well.

Love, I stammer monosyllables.
    The heart's dictionary
Falls from my fingers. Tender vocables
Are crying out. We are the lock and key.

CHANNEL PORT NIGHT

    Boats signal nothing but night.
This English Channel port town is only eyes
Of green and red and yellow. Tide is in.
Waves keep calm. Only the gulls' cries
Insist on being heeded. Now we begin
    A dream-voyage under the light

    Of little ships and houses. Being near
The rugged clangour of the anchored ships
Tells us swimmers that our dreams will be
Constant with voyages. Love, I touch your lips
And taste their salt. Do the same now to me
    Before the night's *détour*.

A WEATHER SPELL

Seven times seven and seven again,
Come the wind and come the rain,
Come the snow and come the heat
And come where darts of lightning meet.

Come all weather, come all ways
To join and part or walk a maze.
Come, my love, be light to start.
Let no thunder break your heart.

I will take the elements
And move their dangerous charges. Chance
Is tossed away. I give you choice
And a purpose and a voice.

I will take the dark aside,
Make the furious seas divide,
But most I'll breach the wall of you
Come the heat and come the snow.

THOUGHT AND FEELING

I have grown wary of the ways of love
And when I find a moment crammed with thought
I cherish that sweet coolness and I move

As only spirits can, as dryads caught
In a Greek grove, then loosed among the trees.
Worship does not mean passion, I was taught.

But I have been brought down upon my knees
Was it by prayer or by the ancient church
In which I found both art and artifice?

I do not know but I know I must touch
And that it is by flesh the spirit lives.
The strides of mind are prisoned in the reach

Of sense so intricate that it receives
All impressions, sieves them as a beach
Takes worn-down, random stones and offers them

To any wanderer there on his way home.

I COUNT THE MOMENTS

I count the moments of my mercies up,
I make a list of love and find it full.
I do all this before I fall asleep.

Others examine consciences. I tell
My beads of gracious moments shining still.
I count my good hours and they guide me well

Into a sleepless night. It's when I fill
Pages with what I think I am made for,
A life of writing poems. Then may they heal

The pain of silence for all those who stare
At stars as I do but are helpless to
Make the bright necklace. May I set ajar

The doors of closed minds. Words come and words go
And poetry is pain as well as passion.
But in the large flights of imagination

I see for one crammed second, order so
Explicit that I need no more persuasion.

LOVE NEEDS AN ELEGY

Move over into your own secrecy.
The planet cools. Our bodies lie apart.
I am not part of you, nor you of me,

We have a separate and a wounded heart,
We hear the world, we see the kings go by
And men and children happy from the start.

Why are they so or is it all a lie?
Listen, a wind is rising. I think spring
Is skirmishing today. It feels nearby

Yet we are not affected. I hear wings
And flights. The birds need never heed the clock
Or hear a lonely summons. Such light sings

But we fit nowhere. What is it can break
Hearts while there's good faith still? I do not know;
We keep our promises but stay awake.

If love could be a matter of the will
O this would never be most sadly so.

ON ITS OWN

Never the same and all again.
Well, no same loss will tear me through
Or the same pain grip me if you
Go on your way. I yet shall gain
Knowledge and never wish unknown
The arguments that reach the bone,

The feelings which lay waste the heart.
No tidy place, no, I will have
All the destructiveness of love
If I can know, beyond the hurt,
Happiness waits or partly so
But not like once and long ago.

My world shall be dramatic then,
No repetitions, many acts,
A few hard treaties, broken tracts,
And peace made stronger yet by pain
Accepted but not chosen when
Love is its own and not again.

DEATH

They did not speak of death
But went round and round the subject deviously.
They were out of breath
With keeping it at bay. When would they see
That they were burdened with

Dying like other men?
Immediate mourners know the whole of grief
When they've seen the dying in pain
And the gradual move toward the end of life.
O death comes again and again

And starts with the crying child and the doctor's knife.

AN ELUSIVE ONE

You slipped away but left your ghost.
Did you expect me, then, to trust
Hauntings like that? I sent them off.
I want no counterfeits of love.

You play me false. Why would you be
That cold, elusive one? I see
No point in indirectness. Say
What your game is. Why do you play

So deviously? Come full, come clear
As out will come a shouldering star
With only one way to be seen.
Are you so unsure who you are?

HAUNTED HOUSE

The house was haunted yet the dwellers there
   Could never run away.
They were accustomed to its chilly air
   And felt calm during day.

It was the night which was their warder and
   Kept them locked within
Half-fear, half-curiosity. A wind,
A draught, then quiet and now ghosts would begin

Their little tappings, moans and then a cry.
   The dwellers lay still then.
Why do we waste time thinking, 'Who next dies?'
Or feel with ghosts half pleasure and half pain?

SPIRITS

If there are spirits, then they breathe in birds
Tossed by the winds, agile in the frost.
Though the world falls down like a house of cards,
Spirits will soar and in birds put their trust
Who rely on us to feed them as we must

In lengthy winters like the last; it is
Our happy task to keep these fliers going,
To give them nuts and crumbs. When it is snowing
They huddle in the evergreens and press
Their lean, bright breasts upon that lastingness.

But if there are, say, angels, or the Greek
Nymphs, and though it is a fancy to
Speculate, it's thus we like to speak.
Who could believe a nearly dead thing flew
As cold blackbirds so frequently will do?

These are approximations but they touch
As near as men can through the boundaries
Rounding our senses' exploration. Much
Is still mysterious, but man probes and tries
To halt a hope, a fragment where it lies,

A vestige of his dreams. If he lets go
Of it he cannot live. Our dreams express
Acts we daren't do. But let mankind be slow
To lose the impulse of their images.
Releasing them, they'll let so much more go.

THE DANGEROUS ONES

We are the silences you dread so much,
We are the agonizing pauses when
You need to speak. We are the final touch,
    We are acutest pain.

But we are more. We do not come and go
And there is nothing which alleviates
The ache, the bleeding. We are tears which flow
    Through your own eyes' gates.

We look with care for victims, never fail
To find the one who'll catch our sickness worst.
If any tell you this is an old tale,
    Look out, they are the first

Of our whole army. They will weaken you,
Paint you pallid, slowly make you move
Until you limp. We are the acts you do
    That never looked at love.

SPELL OF THE ELEMENTS

Fire and water, air and earth
Contend, unite. A magic birth
Is taking place somewhere not far
Celebrated by a star.

Take the music of the wind,
Take the fingers of a mind
Making, breaking, letting go.
Take the blanket of the snow

And a necklace of the stars,
Take the footsteps of the hours.
All can spell-bind, all can build,
All will come if you have called.

We are subject to a spell.
It is married to free-will.
Come the spring, the earth will lie
Lucky under lucky sky.

No determinism has
Power to hold us long. We pass
Into every element,
Come and gone but never spent.

A CHORUS OF CREATION

With hands and with fingers, with trailing of these in the high
Seas, on the first rock rising and on the first
Bird escaping, taking air on its back,
Carrying a branch and riding up, up,
Up to the still molten sky, across the arteries
Of air and the winds' currents—

Event after event,
Establishment of rules,
Then time suggested, only suggested by
The fall of a drop of quintessential life
On a looming rock. Then, then at last
Breath bringing life, drawing a bud up,
Putting it into the light, light which was air,
All that metal dissolved.

The breath is a force, is also a tremor of music,
Notes taken later up by birds who fall
Into different flights according to their size.
And hands, the rudimentary hands are searching,
Under the water, over the life now going
Up with green breath into a morning sky,
The first dawn dancing, the first clouds passing by.

A CHORUS

Over the surging tides and the mountain kingdoms,
Over the pastoral valleys and the meadows,
Over the cities with their factory darkness,
Over the lands where peace is still a power,
Over all these and all this planet carries
A power broods, invisible monarch, a stranger
To some, but by many trusted. Man's a believer
Until corrupted. This huge trusted power
Is spirit. He moves in the muscle of the world,
In continual creation. He burns the tides, he shines
From the matchless skies. He is the day's surrender.
Recognize him in the eye of the angry tiger,
In the sigh of a child stepping at last into sleep,
In whatever touches, graces and confesses,
In hopes fulfilled or forgotten, in promises

Kept, in the resignation of old men—
This spirit, this power, this holder together of space
Is about, is aware, is working in your breathing.
But most he is the need that shows in hunger
And in the tears shed in the lonely fastness.
And in sorrow after anger.

AN EDUCATION

How rooted this was in
Concrete matters, purposes of time
And nightly circumstance.
If this was visionary, then it was
Not won and not expected.
I'd rather see it as a part of learning
And none of it prepared.

At ten years old, I walked out to the night
In an Oxford suburb not yet spoilt
By hurried building. Fields grew at my back,
And in the evergreens of a front garden
I moved without the fear of shadows or
Any interruption. Then I stared
Up at a sky surely spawning stars
Or was the moon releasing one by one
Her young? Or was the firmament so crammed
With precious stones it gave a few away?

I do not know but what I still store in
The corner of a memory of clutter
Of intellectual bric-à-brac, is this—
The memory of elation, changing too,
Being elevated into wonder
Unknown before. The atmosphere was charged
And so was I. My ten years fell away
As I was caught up in an education
Sublime and starry. Maybe all of this
Lasted no more than seconds, but it stayed
With me, a keepsake for the harder years.
A child I was of moods like many children,
And like them in this strange illumination.
But number does not count nor vanity.
I am a wanderer still among those stars.

A NEW PATIENCE

He warms his hands at artificial heat
    And puts a blanket round
His legs. He does not want to drink or eat,
He is content with this new sleeping sound

Close by. She fell asleep before he had
    Finished last kisses but he,
With knowledge he hadn't learnt, left her in bed,
And now he is a full discovery
To his own self. The terrible prison years

He can shrug off. Love was an hour ago
    But he is patient and
As purposeful as a sun-dial which can show
The garden darkening on its rigid hand.

EUTHANASIA

The law's been passed and I am lying low
Hoping to hide from those who think they are
Kindly, compassionate. My step is slow.
I hurry. Will the executioner
Be watching how I go?

Others about me clearly feel the same.
The deafest one pretends that she can hear.
The blindest hides her white stick while the lame
Attempt to stride. Life has become so dear.
Last time the doctor came,

All who could speak said they felt very well.
Did we imagine he was watching with
A new deep scrutiny? We could not tell.
Each minute now we think the stranger Death
Will take us from each cell

For that is what our little rooms now seem
To be. We are prepared to bear much pain,
Terror attacks us wakeful, every dream
Is now a nightmare. Doctor's due again.
We hold on to the gleam

Of sight, a word to hear. We act, we act,
And doing so we wear our weak selves out.
We said 'We want to die' once when we lacked
The chance of it. We wait in fear and doubt.
O life, you are so packed

With possibility. Old age seems good.
The ache, the anguish—we could bear them we
Declare. The ones who pray plead with their God
To turn the murdering ministers away,
But they come softly shod.

THE WRONG SUBJECT

So many interests you had. You needed all
To quench your curiosity. I too
Would have a hand in more than the quickening feel
Of prosody. I grew up much like you,
But your wish was to heal,

Or rather study man. Anatomy
Would have made your whole life much happier
But you, wanting to marry, chose to be
A guardian of public health. You were
Good at it, but I see,

Years later, that your craving for a kind
Of study which you loved had made of you
A nervous man, swift to be angry, lined
Too young. I had the luck to find the true
End to ambition, combined

The abstract and the concrete, caught from you
The love of taking things apart and learning
New possibilities. I wish I knew,
Or had known earlier, frustrations turning
Your life slantwise. Words go

As doctor's eyes should to the quick of life.
Words heal the user. It needs gentle hands
To dare to touch sick bodies. Surely if
You'd had man's bones to love, there'd been less grief.
Doctors like poets move to the same ends.
It's largely luck which mends and understands.

SOME NEVER FORGOTTEN WORDS
OF MY MOTHER'S

'You'll end a murderer'—
The words shiver and thrill me through today.
I was six years old and kicking a door,
     Trying to get my way.

     You, so gentle, were
Yet adamant in this and rightly so.
     You've left me with a fear
Of losing my rash rage, not letting go

     All laws. Yet temper still
Rages in me occasionally and,
     When it does, I feel
A door rise up and kept locked by your hand.
     Then my still untamed will

     Pushes for some small
Favour I have no right to or, perhaps
     Half-want, yes, to kill
A petty stranger. Mother, you've laid traps
     And you protect me still.

THE GARDENS STRETCH

The gardens stretch, happy under a sun
Cantering through the day. It puts its hands
On me and guides me. All the dark has gone
And snow has melted. That stark winter ends

And so does our imprisonment. Why did
I pause today, as if I'd come upon
A life I did not understand? What led
Me through the woken stems, the spacious sun,

The long debate of seasons we do not
Become accustomed to? It's good we don't.
Freshness rides us. We are gladly caught

In trances of the light and dark. We can't
Choose, as we can choose an abstract thought.
We're beggars always, yet glad of our want.

SUMMER SCENE

Air through a window only, but
   It carried with it scents
Of grass and trees and also caught
   The South with that intense,

Authentic charge, so hot, so strong.
   Time is defeated by
Potent reminders which belong
   Also to that starred sky

Fixed but dazzling. Night comes on
   Slowly, but sitters here
Surrender to the pacific moon
   And that air still, that air.

SEA SONG

Listen, the palm trees shake
   In a quick concern of wave.
Hear the breakers make
   New music and now have

An invisible orchestra of
   Sounds to purify
Our lives and make us love
   A little before we die.

Shall we speak or shall
   We let the silence be
As obedient as a shell
   Which stores the voice of the sea?

Well, let the children say
   Their wishes while we are
Only the night and day,
   Only the sun or a star.

SEA-DRUNK

    Acquaint me with some grief
For I am walking half between the air
    And land. There is relief
In feeling thus and having now no share
    Of gravity. This life

    Suits me best when I
Can't see or hear a clock. My roots have come
Up, I am like the gulls which dignify
    The tired shore. My home
Is half with sea, the other half with sky.

When sleep appears I'll drown yet stay alive,
    The diver and the dive.

SPRING TWILIGHT

This is that good hour when
The dying twitterings of several birds
Speak, but in a lower strain
Of spring wrought of suggestions moving towards
A world of etched trees, all in silhouette
As the pale, drained sky shows the sun has set.

One window in my room
Is open to the warmth that channels through
Shafts of coldness. I have come
Into a season and all acts I do
Are steeped in gold, royal authority.
I am the shadow locked into that tree

A dozen yards away.
I am the new moon pencilled on the sky
And I am my whole yesterday,
But most I am this moment, am held by
Its crystal dome around me. When it's night
I shall be all the scattered stars in sight.

And as I stare around
My room, it interests me with shadows of
Ruled, careful lines, a geometry
But also an old exercise of love,
Shaped partly of a spirit quick to take
Colour from climate. When it is daybreak

The moment's clarity will sunder and
I'll take the sun's white wafer on my hand.

NIGHT MOMENT

One cedar tree, one oak, one sycamore
    Turn in a little sigh
Of wind. This is the day's evasive hour,
    For now the quick-change sky

Is restive, paling, sinking, letting go,
    Her anchor pulls away.
Moment by moment all the trees will show
    A branch of stars to stay

Until the morning. Under those stars sleep
    Or at least lie peacefully.
All bird-calls have just stopped. Our world dreams deep
    And for ten hours is free.

NIGHT POWER

Am I alone now as the wind comes up
Sweeping huge stretches of the darkened sky,
Threading the stars, enfolding others' sleep?

I am yet am not. In this room that's high
Above a formal garden far away
From crowds and noise, I am the lonely cry

Of owls who tell the hours. I rule the day
As my mind reaches for before-dawn peace
And there is reason in the words I say

Or write. How warm it is. The bluff winds sing
The rise in temperature. I think the end
Of winter's come, but now is neither spring

Nor any other season while I stand,
As if the globe were trembling in my hand
And I could still the world's fraught whispering.

THE APT PHRASE

To have the apt phrase now and then
But O so much more then than now.
There is rain tapping on a pane
   Of glass. I would teach how
   To be punctilious with words
As clouds are when they forecast rain.
I'd have instinctive flights from birds,
   I would feel any pain

If cadences were at my beck
If images conveyed my drift.
   Where is the one poem I can make?
   How many words are left?

A PROUSTIAN MOMENT

It wasn't a moment. It
Was not possessed by time. Just now a shaft
Of broad sun shone and set
All Rome before me caught in memory's net.
I wish I knew the craft

Of Proustian moments when
Five senses link and smell is what we see,
Light is heard. Again
Touch could strike lightnings in that April rain
And Rome was palpably

About me, all the great
Churches and ruins rose in the bread-sweet air.
How do we open the gate
To this? We cannot, we can only wait
Until again we hear

Nostalgic powers making us surrender
All but attention and an ancient wonder.

A CHINESE POEM

It may be hot. This picture does not show
Though in the centre water's coursing down
Rapids from a river we can't see.
Not far from the horizon is a bridge,
An old man leans on it. Whether he is
Wise we do not know.

Nor do we know if those two close together
And yet not touching, under a willow tree
Have reached the end or start of love. It is,
The painter seems to say, not our affair.

The old man's wisdom and the couple's passion
Are left in doubt but what we learn from these
Cautiously offered, careful objects is
That things remain themselves. The rapids flow
Whether a wise man notices or not.
That willow droops but does not weep for these

Lovers. We need reminders now and then,
We, ardents for pathetic fallacies.
What matters is that water will stay cool
If lovers suffer or that man's a fool.

BRAQUE'S DREAM

You are in a wood and you can hear
    Music playing far off.
Violins are singing, you are sure
    And there are sounds enough

For your exploring. You will take apart
    These violins, these trees,
And from some strength which struggles in your heart
    You will refashion these

Shapes and sounds and, with a quiet shade
    Of brown will tell us more
Of two great arts. A masterpiece is made
    And the world was different before.

CHRISTMAS SUITE IN FIVE MOVEMENTS

1. The Fear

So simple, very few
Can be so bare, be open to the wide
Dark, the starless night, the day's persistent
Wearing away of time. See, men cast off
Their finery and lay it on the floor,

Here, of a stable. What do they wait for?
Answers to learned questions? No, they have
Been steeped in books and wear the dust of them.

Philosophy breaks all its definitions,
Logic is lost, and here
The Word is silent. This God fears the night,
A child so terrified he asks for us.
God is the cry we thought came from our own
Perpetual sense of loss.
Can God be frightened to be so alone?
Does that child dream the Cross?

2. *The Child*

Blood on a berry,
   Night of frost.
Some make merry.
   Some are lost.

Footsteps crack
   On a pool of ice.
Hope is back.
   This baby lies

Wrapped in rags,
   Is fed by a girl.
O if God begs,
   Then we all hold

Him in our power.
   We catch our breath.
This is the hour
   For the terrible truth,

Terrible, yes,
   But sweet also.
God needs us.
   Now, through snow,

Tomorrow through heat
   We carry him
And hear his heart
   And bring him home.

3. *A Litany*

Mary of solace, take our hope,
Girl untouched, take our hands,
Lady of Heaven, come to our homes,
You bring Heaven down.

Mary of mercy, learn our laws,
Lady of care, take impulse to
Your heart, give us grace,
More than enough
And a relish for
The renewal of love.

Queen of formal gardens, reach our forests,
Girl of the fountains, come into our desert.
Mary of broken hearts, help us to keep
Promises. Lady of wakefulness, take our sleep.
You hold God in your arms and he may weep.

4. *The Despair*

All night you fought the dream and when you woke
Lay exhausted, blinded by the sun.
How could you face the day which had begun?
As we do, Christ, but worse for you. You broke
Into our history. History drives you on.

Love before this was dust, but it was dust
You took upon yourself. Your empty hands
Have scars upon them. You have made amends
For all wrong acts, for love brought down to lust.
God, the world is crying and man stands

Upon the brink of worse than tragedy.
That was noble. Now there's something more
Than careful scenes and acts. Some men make war
On you and we feel helpless, are not free
To struggle for you. God, we've seen you poor

And cold. Are stars dispensing light that you
Should find the universe turned . . . can it be
Away from you? No, no, we cannot see
Far or fully. Christ, just born, you go
Back to the blighted, on to the thriving Tree.

5. *The Victory*

Down to that littleness, down to all that
Crying and hunger, all that tiny flesh
And flickering spirit—down the great stars fall,
Here the huge kings bow.
Here the farmer sees his fragile lambs,
Here the wise man throws his books away.

This manger is the universe's cradle,
This singing mother has the words of truth.
Here the ox and ass and sparrow stop,
Here the hopeless man breaks into trust.
God, you have made a victory for the lost.
Give us this daily Bread, this little Host.